Families Work and

by Linda B. Ross

The people in a family do many things together.

They work together.
They have fun together, too.

Families work together
in many ways.

Pam's family makes dinner.
Everyone helps. Pam sets
the table. Todd helps, too.
He makes the salad.

Ellie works in the garden.
She helps her grandmother
and grandfather plant flowers.

Ben and his family wash the car together.
They like to keep it clean.

Ted and his dad wash the car.
They keep their car clean.
Now Ted and his dad are clean!

Families have fun together, too.
Janna's family likes to go swimming.

They are having fun!

Jon and his grandfather like to fix bikes.

Jon's family takes
long rides together.

Kim and her mom
play games together.
Kim likes to win.
So does her mom!

Families work and play together.
They like to be together.